E S T A T E   P U B L I C A T I O N S

BASINGSTOKE
ANDOVER

ALTON · HEATH END · KINGSCLERE
OAKLEY · OVERTON · TADLEY
WHITCHURCH

G000123600

ROAD MAP Page 2
BASINGSTOKE CENTRE Page 3
INDEX TO STREETS Page 28

Kingsclere 14

Tadley

Chineham 6 7

Houndmills 4 5 Popley

Winklebury Old Basing

Overton 16 15 Oakley South Ham 3 10 11

Penton Mewsey 20 Knights Enham 21 22 23

Charlton Walworth

17 Whitchurch

8 9 BASINGSTOKE

Kempshott 11

Hatch Warren

ANDOVER
24 25 26 27

Anna Valley

18 19
ALTON

One-way Street →
Car Park 🅿
Place of Worship ✛
Post Office ●
Public Convenience ⧆
Pedestrianized ▨

Scale of street plans 4 inches to 1 mile
Unless otherwise stated

Street plans prepared and published by ESTATE PUBLICATIONS, Bridewell House, TENTERDEN, KENT, and based upon the ORDNANCE SURVEY maps with the sanction of the Controller of H. M. Stationery Office.

The publishers acknowledge the co-operation of Basingstoke & Deane Borough Council, and Test Valley Borough Council in the preparation of these maps.

MAP 5

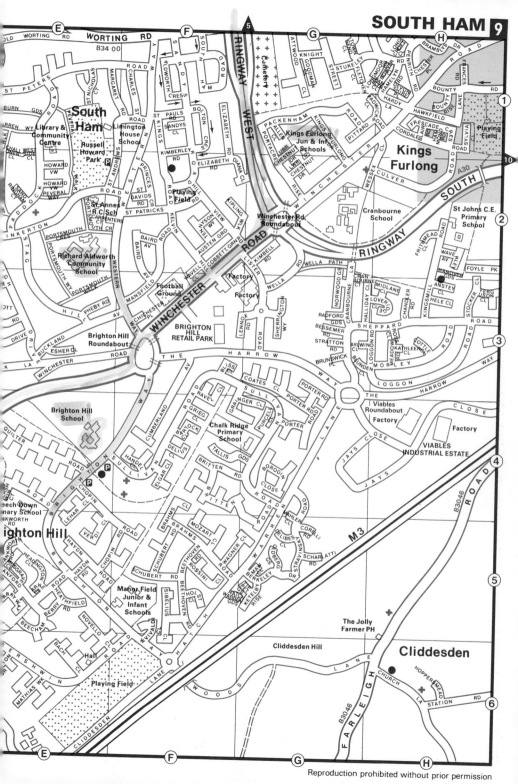

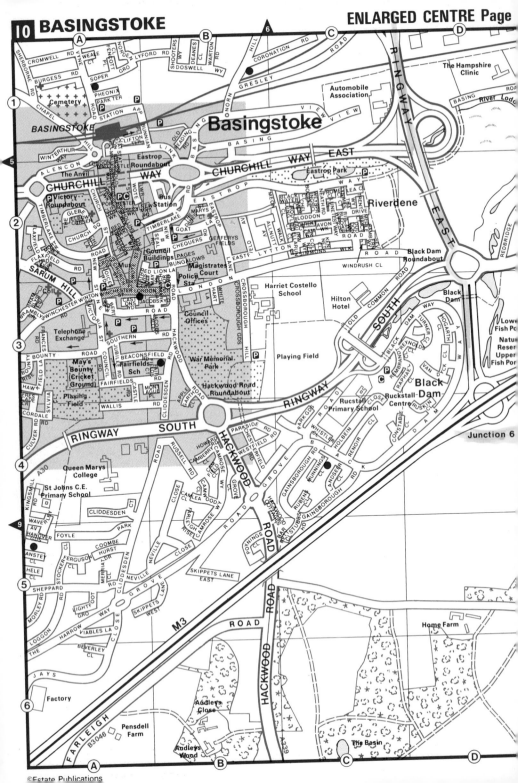

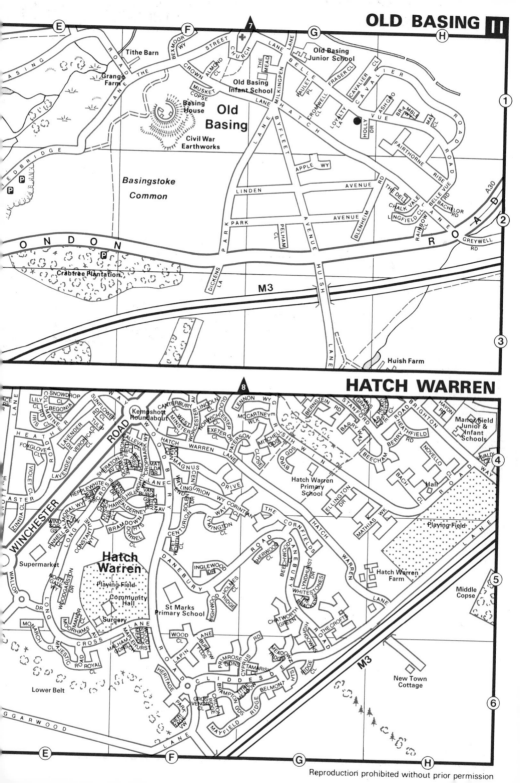

HATCH WARREN

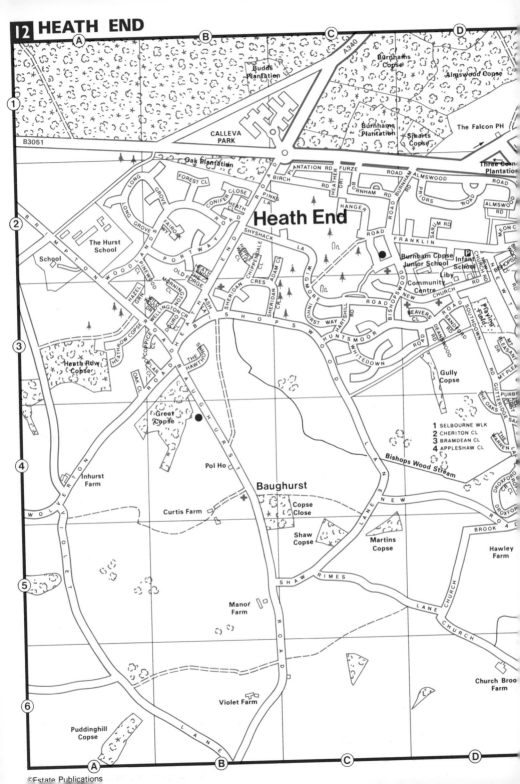

Heath End

Baughurst

1 SELBOURNE WLK
2 CHERITON CL
3 BRAMDEAN CL
4 APPLESHAW CL

Bishops Wood Stream

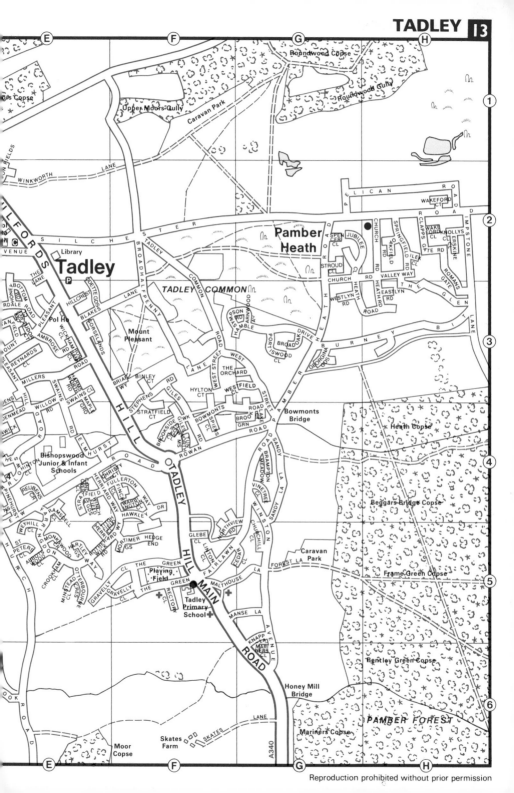

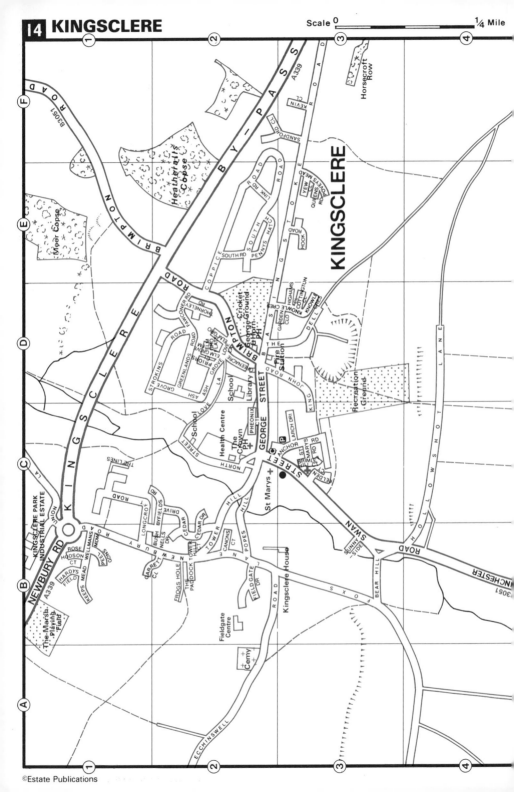

Scale 0   ¼ Mile

KINGSCLERE

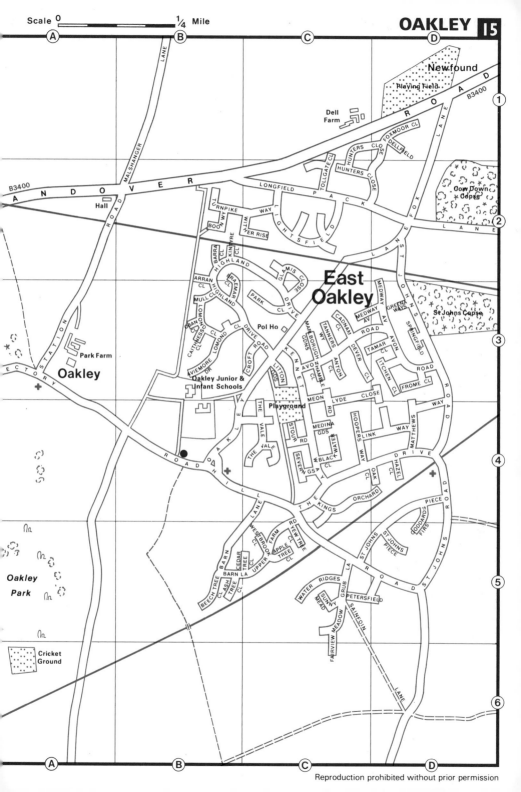

Scale 0 ¼ Mile

Newfound

Playing Field

B3400

Dell Farm

FOXMOOR CL

DELLFIELD

HUNTERS CLOSE

TOLLGATE CL

HUNTERS CLOSE

Cow Down Copse

B3400

A N D O V E R

MALSHANGER LANE

LONGFIELD

PACK LANE

LIGHTSFIELD

FOX LANE

Hall

TURNPIKE WY

BOO

WILL MYER RISE

WAY

BARRA CL

HIGHLAND

KINTYRE CL

GLAMIS CLOSE

PARK DRIVE

East Oakley

JOHNS WAY

MEDWAY AV

ST JOHNS

GREEN WAYS

St Johns Copse

ARRAN CL

BRAEMAR CL

HIGHLAND

MULL CL

OBAN CL

CAITHNESS

CLYNE

LOMOND CL

AVIEMORE DR

HIGHLAND CL

DRIVE

CROFT ROAD

Pol Ho

KENNET

MARLBOROUGH GDNS

NETHAME

TANNERS WY

CADNAM CL

ANTON CL

DEVER CL

MEDWAY AV

TAMAR CL

ITCHEN CL

ROAD

AVON

SPRINGFIELD

ROAD

FROME CL

STATION

Park Farm

Oakley

RECTORY

Oakley Junior & Infant Schools

LITTON GDS

AVON CLOSE

LYDE CLOSE

MEON

WAY

MATTHEWS

Playground

THE VALE

THE VALE

STOUR RD

MEDINA GDS

SEVERN

WATER CL

BLAC GSP

HOOPERS WAY

LINK

WAY

DRIVE

HAZEL CL

OAK CL

KILN

ROAD

OAK HILL LANE

THE KINGS

ORCHARD

ST JOHNS PIECE

GODDARDS FIRS

PIECE

ST JOHNS ROAD

Oakley Park

WESTBROOK

BARN

CEDAR TREE

ASH TREE

UPPER FARM

APPLE TREE CL

YEW TREE RD

ST JOHNS LA

BEECH TREE

BARN LA

WATER RIDGES

SUN WEAD

GRUB

Petersfield

FAIRVIEW MEADOW

SAINFOIN

Cricket Ground

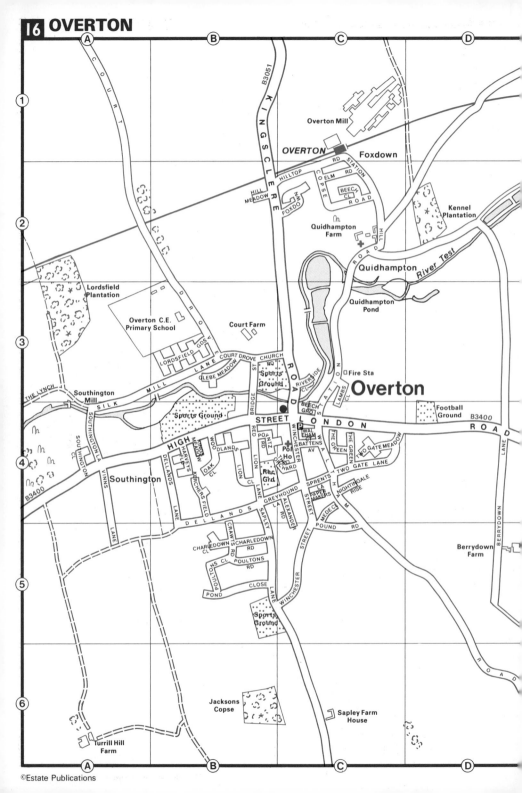

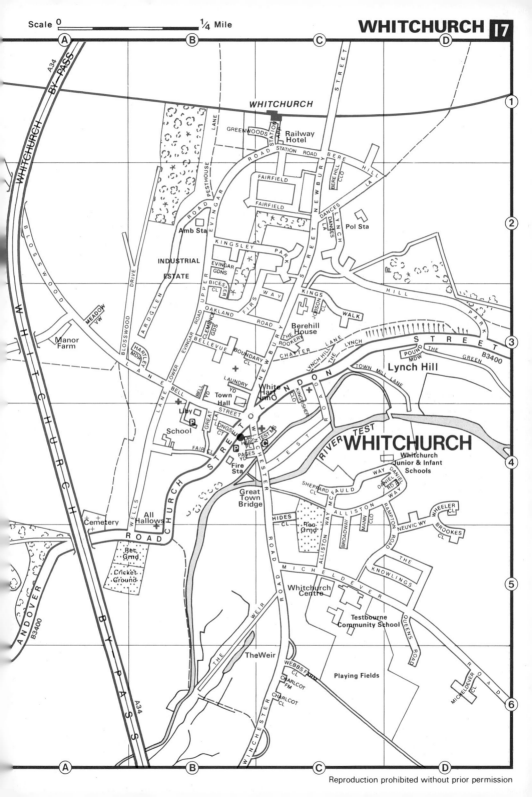

Scale 0 ¼ Mile

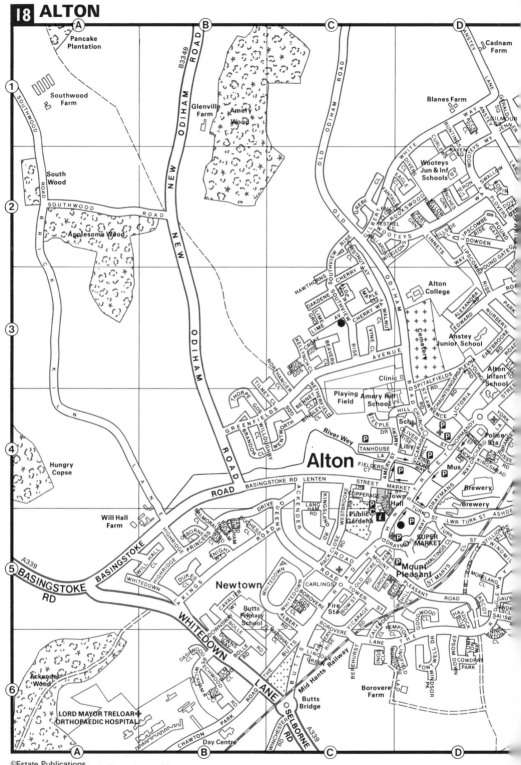

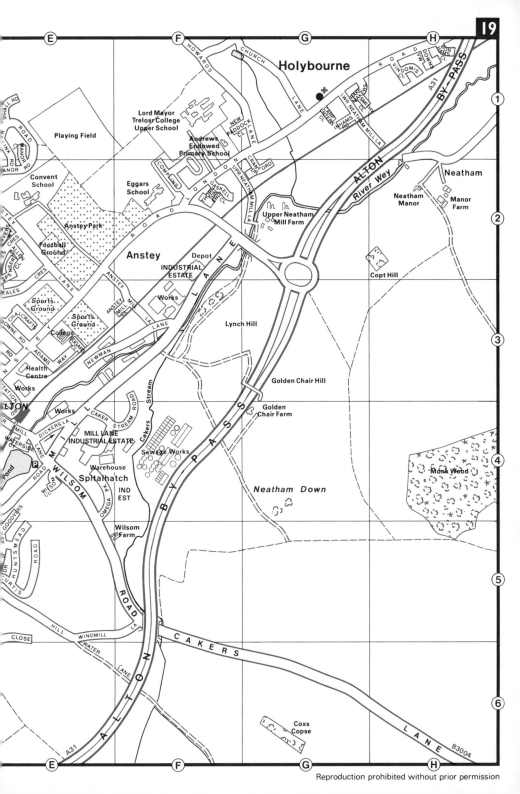

E F G H

Holybourne

ROAD
VINDOMIS CL
A31
ALTON BY PASS
FERNS
VINDOMIS CL
DOWN
CL
SMITHS
JESMOND CL

(1)

Lord Mayor
Treloar College
Upper School

NEW
PADDOCK
CL

CHURCH LANE
HOWARDS

LWR NEATHAM MILL LA
WINHAMS
LA

Playing Field

Andrews
Endowed
Primary School

COMPAINS

UPR NEATHAM MILL LA

CRANFORD

Neatham

Convent
School

Eggars
School

GASKELL
HOTON CL

Upper Neatham
Mill Farm

Neatham
Manor

Manor
Farm

ALTON
River Wey

(2)

Anstey Park

MANOR RD
KINGS RD
KINGSHALL RD

STEVENS CRES
ALLEN SPENSERS CL
CRES
BEALES

Anstey

Depot
INDUSTRIAL
ESTATE

Copt Hill

Football
Ground

Sports
Ground

CHALCRAFTS
TOWNE RD

ANSTEY MILL LA
ANSTEY MILL LA

Works

Lynch Hill

(3)

Sports
Ground

College

ADAMS WAY
EGGARS

NEWMAN

BY PASS

Golden Chair Hill

Health
Centre
Works

Golden
Chair Farm

(4)

LTON

Works
Works

DICKERS LA
CAKER STREAM ROAD

MILL LANE
INDUSTRIAL ESTATE

Cakers Stream

Sewage Works

Monk Wood

MILL LANE
WATERSIDE

Pond

WILSOM

Warehouse
Spitalhatch

IND
EST

OMEGA PK

Neatham Down

WILSON CL

Wilsom
Farm

(5)

ROAD

HUNTSMEAD
GOODYERS
CURTIS

CLOSE

HILL
WINDMILL
WATER LANE
LA

CAKERS

Coxs
Copse

(6)

A31
ALTON

B3004

LANE

E F G H

Reproduction prohibited without prior permission

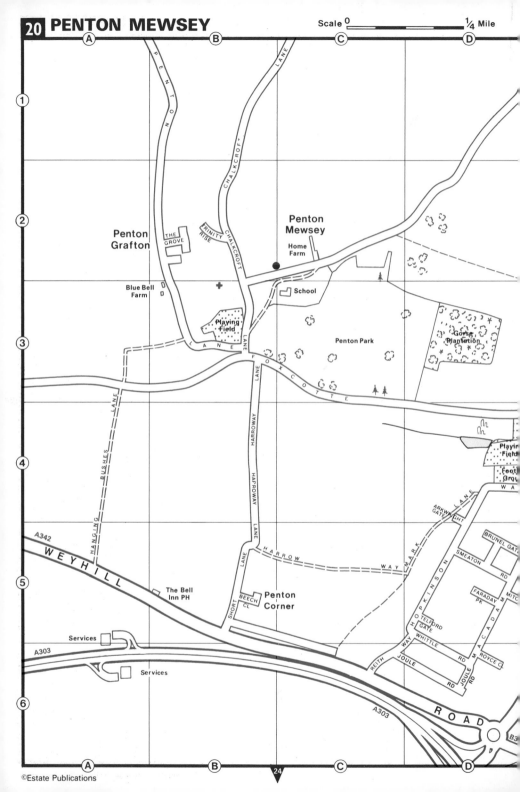

Scale 0 ¼ Mile

PENTON

CHALKCROFT LANE

Penton
Grafton

THE GROVE

TRINITY RISE

CHALKCROFT LANE

**Penton
Mewsey**

Home
Farm

Blue Bell
Farm

School

Playing
Field

Penton Park

LANE

LANE

FOXCOTTE

Gorse
Plantation

BUSHES LANE

HANGING

HARROWAY LANE

HARROWAY LANE

A342

WEYHILL

The Bell
Inn PH

SHORT LANE

BEECH CL

HARROW WAY

**Penton
Corner**

MARK

ARKWRIGHT
GATE

Playir
Field

Foot
Grou

W A

BRUNEL GATE

SMEATON RD

FARADAY PK

MITC

HOPKINSON WAY

TELFORD
GATE

MACADAM

RD

ROYCE C

Services

A303

Services

REITH

JOULE

WHITTLE WAY

JOULE RD

JOULE RD

RD

ROAD

A303

B3

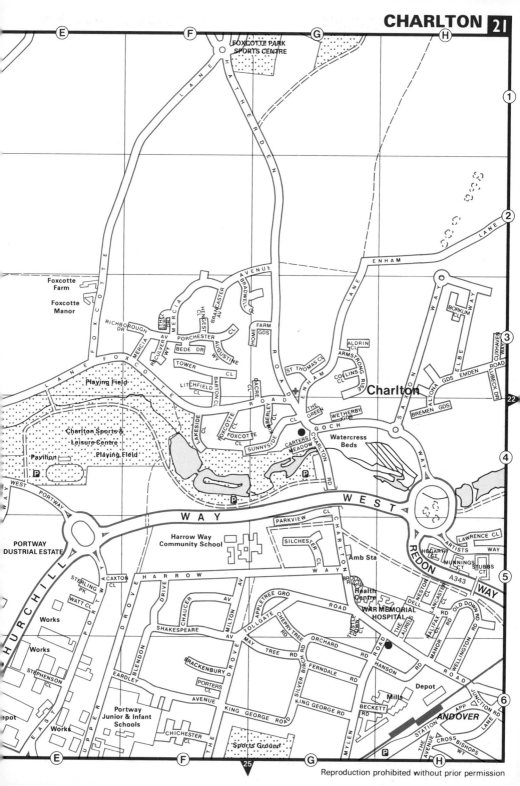

KNIGHTS ENHAY
INFANTS SCHOOL

Finkley Down
Farm Park

Works

Works

Works

The Icknield
School

Engineering
Works

WALWORTH
INDUSTRIAL ESTATE

Depot

Sports Ground

Factory

Central Way

Factory

Crown Wy

West Way

Works

Works

Works

Factory

Works

Flinders Cl

Works

Factory

Queen
Charlotte PH

Vigo Junior &
Infant Schools

Norman
School

laying Field

WAY

CHURCHILL

WAY

A3093

LONDON

ROAD

B3400

London Rd

Reproduction prohibited without prior permission

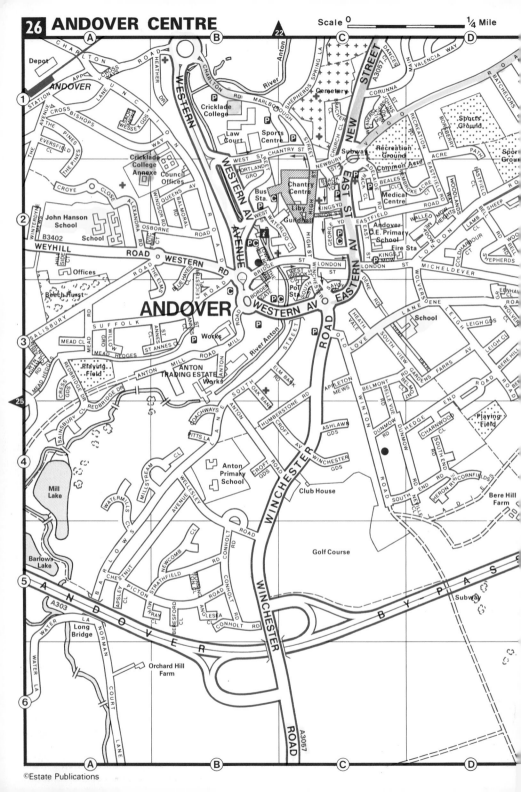

23

Handwritten note
1st PART OF TRIP
VIGO SCHOOL

Map labels

E **F** **G** **H**

B3400 ROAD

CHURCHILL WAY
A3093

COLUMBUS WAY
SCOTT CL.
OX DROVE

Junior & Schools

Playing Field

The Winton School

JOHN ST
NAPIER WK
NELSON WK
SOMER
JERVIS
BENBOW
ADMIRALS
DUNCAN
BEATTY
BOSCAWEN
FISHER
ADMIRALS W
HOOD CL
HOWE CL

Queen Charlotte PH

LONDON
LONDON ROAD

WINTON
HIGHLANDS
MOUTH RD
GRO LANDS
PEN CL
RD

STILES DR
PEARMAN
PALMER DR CL
CHASE
SPRINGFIELD CLOSE
CHARLOTTE CL
CLOSE

WALK

PICKET

1

2

Lower Farm

LADIES

Iron Bridge (Footbridge)

ROAD
MICHEL
WOLVERSDEN GDNS

Ashley Court Hotel

WALK

3

Rent Hay Farm

FOREST LANE

TWENTY

ROAD

ANDOVER   BY-PASS
A303

4

Subway

LANE

5

COWDOWN

Cowdown Farm

6

Cowdown Copse

E **F** **G** **H**

race Sq. SP10 22 D4
ranada Pl. SP10 23 E5
aveney Sq. SP10 22 D4
eenhaven Clo. SP10 26 D3
eenwich Way. SP10 22 C4

ackwood Clo. SP10 25 G3
adrian Rd. SP10 22 C3
aig Rd. SP10 25 G1
alifax Clo. SP10 21 H5
amble Ct. SP10 22 D4
ammond Sq. SP10 22 D4
anging Bushes La. SP11 20 A5
anover Clo. SP10 25 F4
anson Rd. SP10 21 H6
arris Clo. SP11 24 C3
arrow Way, Andover. SP10 21 F5
arrow Way, Penton Corner. SP11 20 B5
arrow Way La. SP11 20 B4
awke Clo. SP10 27 F1
atherden Rd. SP10 21 F1
azel Clo. SP10 25 F4
eath Vale. SP10 26 C3
eather Dri. SP10 22 B6
edge End Rd. SP10 26 D4
elford Ct. SP10 22 D4
endren Sq. SP10 22 D4
engest Clo. SP10 21 F3
epworth Clo. SP10 22 B5
eron Rise. SP10 26 D4
gh St. SP10 26 C2
ghbury Rd. SP11 25 G6
ghlands Rd. SP10 27 E2
llbury Av. SP10 25 G3
llside. SP11 24 B6
llside Ct. SP10 26 A2
obbs Sq. SP10 22 D4
ogarth Ct. SP10 21 H5
olmes Ct. SP10 25 G2
ome Farm Gdns. SP10 21 G3
ood Clo. SP10 27 F1
opkinson Way. SP10 20 D5
umberstone Rd. SP10 26 B4
utton Sq. SP10 22 D4

knield Way. SP10 22 C1
NDUSTRIAL ESTATES:
Anton Trading Est. SP10 26 B3
Balksbury Mill Ind Est. SP11 25 G5
Meridian Ind Park. SP10 22 C4
Portway Ind Est. SP10 25 E1
Walworth Ind Est. SP10 23 F5
Westmarch Business Centre. SP10 22 C4

ardine Sq. SP10 22 D4
asmine Ct. SP10 25 G3
ellicoe Ct. .SP10 23 E6
ensen Gdns. SP10 25 G2
ervis Ct. SP10 27 E1
oule Rd. SP10 20 D6
unction Rd. SP10 26 A1

ellys Walk. SP10 25 G2
ennet Ct. SP10 23 E4
ew Walk. SP10 25 G3
mberley Clo. SP10 21 G4
ng Arthurs Way. SP10 22 B3
ng George Rd. SP10 25 F1
ngs Mdw. SP10 26 C2
ings Yard. SP10 26 C2
ngsmead. SP11 25 E6
ngsway. SP10 23 G4

adies Walk. SP10 26 D4
aker Sq. SP10 22 D4
akeside Clo. SP10 21 F4
amb Clo. SP10 26 D2
ancaster Clo. SP10 21 H5
ancelot Clo. SP10 22 B3
andseer Ct. SP10 22 B5
ansdowne Av. SP10 25 G3
arch Dri. SP10 25 E2
arwood Sq. SP10 22 D4
avender Ct. SP10 25 G3
awrence Clo. SP10 21 H5
eicester Pl. SP10 26 B3
eigh Clo. SP10 26 D3
eigh Gdns. SP10 26 D3
eigh Rd. SP10 26 D3
llywhite Cres. SP10 22 C1
me Walk. SP10 25 F3
nton Dri. SP10 22 B5
nwood Dri. SP10 25 G2
chfield Clo. SP10 21 F3

Livingstone Rd. SP10 23 G6
Lock Sq. SP10 23 E4
Lodge Clo. SP10 25 G2
London Rd. SP10 26 D2
London St. SP10 26 C2
Longstock Clo. SP10 25 G3
Love La. SP10 26 C3
Loveridge Clo. SP10 22 C1
Lowry Ct. SP10 22 A5
Lubeck Dri. SP10 21 H3
Lune Ct. SP10 23 E4

Macadam Way. SP10 20 D6
Madrid Rd. SP10 23 E5
Magellan Clo. SP10 23 G6
Magnolia Clo. SP10 25 G3
Majorca Av. SP10 22 D5
Manor Copse. SP10 22 C1
Manor Rise. SP11 25 G6
Manor Road. SP10 21 H6
Maple Walk. SP10 25 F4
March Clo. SP10 22 D5
Marchant Rd. SP10 25 G3
Mark La. SP10 20 D5
Marlborough St. SP10 26 B1
Marshall Sq. SP10 23 E4
May Tree Rd. SP10 21 G6
Mead Clo. SP10 26 A3
Mead Hedges. SP10 26 A3
Meadow Heights. SP10 26 D2
Mead Rd. SP10 26 A3
Meadow Way. SP10 25 F2
Medina Ct. SP10 23 E4
Medway Ct. SP10 23 E4
Meliot Rise. SP10 22 B2
Mercia Av. SP10 21 F3
Mersey Ct. SP10 23 E4
Micheldever Rd. SP10 26 D2
Millstream Clo. SP10 26 A4
Millway Clo. SP10 25 G2
Millway Rd. SP10 25 G2
Milton Av. SP10 21 F5
Mitchell Clo. SP10 20 D5
Monxton Rd. SP10 24 B3
Moore Clo. SP10 22 B5
Moot Clo. SP10 22 C2
Mornington Clo. SP10 26 B5
Mountbatten Ct. SP10 27 E1
Munnings Ct. SP10 21 H5
Murray Clo. SP10 26 A5
Mylen Rd. SP10 25 G1

Napier Walk. SP10 27 E1
Nelson Walk. SP10 27 F1
Nene Ct. SP10 23 E4
Nestor Clo. SP10 21 H5
Neville Clo. SP10 26 D4
New St. SP10 26 C1
Newall Rd. SP11 24 B3
Newbury Rd. SP11 22 C1
Newbury St. SP10 26 C2
Newcombe Clo. SP10 26 B5
Newtown Pl. SP10 25 G2
Norman Court La. SP11 26 A5
North Way. SP10 23 E4
Northern Av. SP10 22 B6

Oak Bank. SP10 26 B3
Olaf Clo. SP10 22 C2
Old Down Rd. SP10 21 H6
Old Winton Rd. SP10 26 C3
Orchard Rd. SP10 21 G6
Orchid Ct. SP10 25 G3
Osborne Rd. SP10 26 A2
Ouse Ct. SP10 23 E4
Ox Drove. SP11 27 G1

Palmer Dri. SP10 27 E2
Parkview Clo. SP10 21 G5
Pattinson Cres. SP11 24 C3
Pearmain Dri. SP10 27 E2
Pembroke Ct. SP10 26 C2
Pen Clo. SP10 27 E2
Penton La. SP10 20 B1
Picket Twenty. SP11 27 G1
Picton Rd. SP10 26 A5
Pilgrims Way. SP10 22 D4
Pine Walk. SP10 25 F4
Pitts La. SP10 26 B4
Plantation Rd. SP10 25 G2
Porchester Clo. SP10 21 F3
Portal Clo. SP11 24 D2
Porters Clo. SP10 21 F6
Portland Gro. SP10 26 B2
Portway Clo. SP10 25 F1
Poynters Clo. SP10 22 A5
Primrose Ct. SP10 25 G3
Prince Clo. SP10 23 E4

Queens Av. SP10 26 B2

Rack Clo. SP10 26 C2
Recreation Rd. SP10 26 D1
Reculver Way. SP10 21 F3
Red Post La. SP11 24 A2
Redbridge Dri. SP10 26 A3
Redon Way. SP10 21 H5
Redrice Rd. SP11 25 G6
Reith Way. SP10 20 C6
Reynolds Ct. SP10 22 A5
Rhodes Sq. SP10 23 E4
Ribble Ct. SP10 23 E4
Richborough Dri. SP10 21 F3
River Way. SP10 22 C5
Robin Way. SP10 22 C4
Rodney Ct. SP10 23 F6
Roman Way. SP10 22 C2
Rooksbury Rd. SP10 25 G3
Roundway Ct. SP10 25 G2
Royce Clo. SP10 20 D6
Ryon Clo. SP10 22 B2

Sainsbury Clo. SP10 26 A4
St Annes Clo. SP10 26 B3
St Hubert Rd. SP10 25 H3
St Johns Rd. SP10 26 C1
St Thomas Clo. SP10 21 G3
Salisbury Rd. SP10 24 D6
Salmond Rd. SP11 24 D2
Savoy Clo. SP10 26 C3
Saxon Ct. SP10 22 B3
Saxon Way. SP10 21 H3
Scott Clo. SP10 23 G6
Severn Ct. SP10 23 E4
Seville Cres. SP10 22 D5
Shackleton Sq. SP10 23 E4
Shakespeare Av. SP10 21 F5
Shannon Ct. SP10 23 E4
Shaw Clo. SP10 25 E2
Sheep Fair. SP10 26 D2
Shepherds Row. SP10 26 D2
Shepherds Spring La. SP10 26 C1
Sheppard Sq. SP10 22 D4
Shoe Mews. SP10 26 A1
Short La. SP11 20 B5
Sidmouth Rd. SP10 27 E2
Silchester Clo. SP10 21 G5
Silk Weavers Rd. SP10 26 C1
Silver Birch Rd. SP10 25 G1
Slessor Clo. SP11 24 D2
Smannell Rd. SP11 22 C4
Smeaton Rd. SP10 20 D5
Sobers Sq. SP10 22 D4
Somerville Ct .SP10 27 F1
South End Rd. SP10 26 C4
South St. SP10 26 B3
South View Gdns. SP10 26 C3
South Way. SP10 23 F5
Spey Ct. SP10 23 E4
Springfield Clo. SP10 27 F1
Spruce Clo. SP10 25 E2
Statham Sq. SP10 23 E3
Station App. SP10 26 A1
Stephenson Clo. SP10 21 E6
Sterling Clo. SP10 21 E5
Stiles Dri. SP10 27 E2
Stourhead Clo. SP10 25 G3
Strathfield Rd. SP10 26 B5
Stuart Ct. SP10 22 C3
Stubbs Ct. SP10 21 H5
Suffolk Rd. SP10 26 A3
Sunnyside Clo. SP10 21 G4
Sutcliffe Sq. SP10 22 D3
Sutherland Ct. SP10 22 B5
Swallowfields. SP10 22 C4
Swift Clo. SP10 22 C4
Sycamore Walk. SP10 25 F4

Taskers Dri. SP11 25 E6
Tate Sq. SP10 22 D3
Tedder Clo. SP11 24 D2
Telford Gate. SP10 20 D5
Test Ct. SP10 23 E4
Thames Ct. SP10 23 E4
The Avenue. SP10 26 A1
The Crescent. SP10 25 E2
The Drove. SP10 25 F2
The Elms. SP10 26 B2
The Firs. SP10 25 G2
The Green. SP10 21 G4
The Grove. SP11 20 B2
The Laurels. SP10 21 H5
The Link. SP10 25 E2
The Mall. SP10 26 B2
The Pines. SP10 26 A1
The Willows. SP10 25 H4
Thistledown Clo. SP10 21 G5
Tiberius Rd. SP10 22 C3
Tintagel Clo. SP10 22 B2
Toledo Gro. SP10 22 D5
Tollgate Rd. SP10 21 G5
Tovey Ct. SP10 23 F6
Tower Clo. SP10 21 F3
Trenchard Rd. SP11 24 D2
Trent Ct. SP10 23 E4
Trinity Rise. SP11 20 B2
Trojan Walk. SP10 22 C3
Trueman Sq. SP10 22 D3
Tudor Ct. SP10 22 C3
Turin Ct. SP10 22 D2
Turner Ct. SP10 22 A5
Tyne Ct. SP10 23 E4

Upper Drove. SP10 25 E1

Valencia Way. SP10 26 D1
Valley Mead. SP11 25 E6
Valley Rise. SP11 25 G6
Venice Ct. SP10 22 D2
Verden Way. SP10 22 A3
Verity Sq. SP10 22 D3
Vespasian Rd. SP10 22 C3
Victoria Ct. SP10 26 B2
Vigo Rd. SP10 26 C1
Viking Way. SP10 22 C2

Walled Meadow. SP10 26 D2
Walnut Tree Rd. SP10 26 A3
Walworth Clo. SP10 23 E5
Ward Clo. SP10 22 B5
Water La. SP11 26 A6
Waterloo Ct. SP10 26 B2
Watermills Clo. SP10 26 A4
Watery La. SP10 22 C5
Watson Acre. SP10 25 G1
Watt Clo. SP10 21 E5
Weavers Clo. SP10 26 C1
Wellesley Rd. SP10 26 B4
Wellington Rd. SP10 21 H6
Wessex Gdns. SP10 26 A1
West Portway. SP10 21 E4
West St. SP10 26 B1
West Way. SP10 23 F5
Westbrook Clo. SP10 26 C2
Western Av. SP10 26 B1
Western Rd. SP10 26 B2
Wetherby Gdns. SP10 21 G4
Weyhill Rd. SP10 25 C1
White Oak Way. SP11 25 E6
Whittle Rd. SP10 20 D5
Whynot La. SP10 25 H1
Willow Gro. SP10 26 A3
Winchester Gdns. SP10 26 C4
Winchester Rd. SP10 26 B4
Winchester St. SP10 26 C2
Windsor Rd. SP10 26 B2
Winterdyne Mews. SP10 26 A2
Winton Chase. SP10 27 E2
Wisley Rd. SP10 25 G3
Wisteria Ct. SP10 25 G3
Witan Clo. SP10 22 C2
Wolversdene Clo. SP10 26 D3
Wolversdene Gdns. SP10 27 E2
Wolversdene Rd. SP10 26 D2
Woodlands Way. SP10 26 D2
Wool Gro. SP10 26 D2
Woolley Sq. SP10 22 D3
Worrell Sq. SP10 22 D3
Wye Ct. SP10 23 E4
Wyndham Rd. SP10 26 A3

York Ct. SP10 22 C3

BASINGSTOKE

Abbey Ct. RG24 5 H1
Abbey Rd. RG24 5 G2
Abbott Clo. RG22 9 E3
Achilles Clo. RG24 7 E1
Aghemund Clo. RG24 6 D1
Ajax Clo. RG24 7 E1
Albert Yd. RG21 3 B4
Albert Wk. RG21 3 B4
Aldermaston Rd. RG24 5 E1
Aldermaston Rd Sth. RG21 5 G3
Alderney Av. RG22 11 F4
Alderwood. RG24 7 E1
Aldworth Cres. RG22 9 F1
Alencon Link. RG21 3 B2
Alexandra Rd. RG21 5 G5
Allen Clo. RG21 9 G1
Alliston Clo. RG22 8 D2
Alliston Way. RG22 8 D2
Allnutt Av. RG21 10 B2
Almond Clo. RG24 11 F1
Alpine Ct. RG22 8 C1
Amport Clo. RG24 7 F4
Anchor Yard. RG21 3 C3
Anglesey Clo. RG24 6 B3
Anstey Clo. RG21 9 H3
Antrim Clo. RG22 8 C2
Applegarth Clo. RG21 3 D5
Apple Way. RG24 11 G2
Arlott Dri. RG21 6 B6
Armstrong Rd. RG24 6 D6
Arne Clo. RG22 9 E5
Arun Ct. RG21 10 C2
Arundel Gdns. RG23 4 D3
Ascension Clo. RG24 6 C3
Ash Gro. RG24 11 H1
Ashfield. RG24 7 E3
Ashwood Way. RG23 5 E3
Aster Rd. RG22 8 B6
Attwood Clo. RG21 5 G6
Augustus Dri. RG23 4 D3
Auklet Clo. RG22 8 A5
Austen Gro. RG22 9 F2
Avon Walk. RG21 10 C2
Aylings Clo. RG23 4 C6
Aylwin Clo. RG21 9 G3

Bach Clo. RG22 9 E6
Bachelor Rd. RG24 11 H2
Badgers Bank. RG24 7 E5
Baird Av. RG22 9 F2
Ballard Clo. RG22 8 D1
Balmoral Ct. RG22 8 D2
Balmoral Way. RG22 11 E5
Bardwell Clo. RG22 8 D1
Barrett Ct. RG21 10 C5
Barron Pl. RG24 4 D2
Barry Way. RG22 9 E5
Bartock Clo. RG22 9 F4
Barton La. RG24 7 E6
Bartons La. RG24 7 F5
Basing Rd. RG24 10 D1
Basing View. RG21 3 D1
Baynard Clo. RG21 6 B6
Beachpiece Way. RG22 11 F4
Beaconsfield Rd. RG21 3 B5
Bear Ct. RG24 7 E6
Beaulieu Ct. RG21 10 C2
Beckett Clo. RG23 4 C6
Bedford Walk. RG21 3 B3
Beech Way. RG23 4 D3
Beecham Berry. RG22 9 E5
Beechwood Clo. RG22 11 F5
Beethoven Rd. RG22 9 F5
Beggarwood La. RG22 11 E6
Begonia Clo. RG22 8 B5
Bell Rd. RG24 6 D6
Belle Vue Rd. RG24 11 G1
Belmont Heights. RG22 11 G6
Belvedere Gdns. RG24 7 F1
Bennet Clo. RG21 6 C6
Berewyk Clo. RG22 11 E4
Berkeley Dri. RG22 9 G5
Bermuda Clo. RG24 6 B3
Bernstein Rd. RG22 8 D5
Berwyn Clo. RG22 8 C2
Bessemer Rd. RG21 9 G3
Beverley Clo. RG22 10 A6
Bexmoor Way. RG24 7 F6
Bilton Rd. RG24 6 D4
Binfields Clo. RG24 7 E4
Birchwood. RG24 7 E1
Bittern Clo. RG22 8 B5
Black Dam Way. RG21 10 C3
Blackberry Walk. RG24 7 E5
Blackbird Clo. RG22 8 A5
Blackdown Clo. RG22 8 C2
Blackthorn Way. RG23 4 D4
Blackwater Clo. RG21 10 C2
Blair Rd. RG21 3 A5
Blenheim Rd. RG24 11 G2
Bliss Clo. RG22 9 F3
Blunden Clo. RG21 9 G3
Bolton Cres. RG22 9 F1
Bond Clo. RG24 6 D4
Borodin Clo. RG22 9 G4
Bounty Rise. RG21 3 A5
Bounty Road. RG21 3 A5
Bourne Ct. RG21 10 C2
Bowman Rd. RG24 7 E1
Bowyer Clo. RG21 5 H5
Boyce Clo. RG22 8 D4
Bracken Bank. RG24 7 E5
Brackley Way. RG22 8 D3
Brahms Clo. RG22 9 F5
Brahms Rd. RG22 9 F5
Bramble Way. RG24 11 H1
Bramblys Clo. RG21 3 A4
Bramblys Dri. RG21 3 A4
Brambling Clo. RG22 8 B5
Bramdown Heights. RG22 11 F5
Brampton Gdns. RG22 11 F6
Branton Clo. RG22 8 D1
Brewer Clo. RG22 8 D1
Brickfields Clo. RG24 7 E5
Brighton Way. RG22 9 E4
Britten Rd. RG22 9 F4

Mahler Clo. RG22 9 G5
Maldive Rd. RG24 6 C3
Malham Gdns. RG22 11 F6
Mallard Clo. RG24 8 A6
Malta Clo. RG24 6 B3
Malvern Clo. RG22 8 C2
Manor Clo. RG22 11E5
Manor La. RG24 7 G6
Mansfield Rd. RG22 9 F3
Mapie Clo. RG22 8 B5
Maple Cres. RG22 6 A5
Maplehurst Chase. RG22 11 F6
Margaret Rd. RG22 9 E1
Marigold Clo. RG22 8 C5
Market Pl. RG21 3 B3
Mark La. RG21 3 C4
Marlowe Clo. RG24 6 B5
Marshall Gdns. RG21 6 B6
Marshcourt. RG24 7 E5
Martin Clo. RG21 6 C5
Martins Wood. RG24 7 E2
Mathias Walk. RG22 9 E6
Matilda Dri. RG22 11 F4
Mattock Way. RG24 6 D2
Maw Clo. RG22 9 G5
May Clo. RG24 11 H1
May Pl. RG21 3 C3
May St. RG21 5 G5
Maybrook. RG24 7 E1
Mayfield Ridge. RG22 11 F6
Mayflower Clo. RG24 6 D2
McCartney Walk. RG22 8 D5
Meadow Ridge. RG22 11 G6
Meadow Rd. RG21 9 H3
Meadowland. RG24 6 D2
Medway Ct. RG21 10 C2
Melford Gdns. RG22 8 B2
Melrose Walk. RG22 5 G2
Mendip Clo. RG22 8 C2
Meon Walk. RG21 10 C2
Mercer Clo. RG22 4 D6
Merriat Clo. RG21 10 A5
Merrileas Gdns. RG22 8 C4
Merrydown La. RG24 7 E1
Merryfield. RG24 6 D2
Merton Rd. RG21 5 G4
Middleton Gdns. RG21 6 D6
Midlane Clo. RG21 9 H3
Milkingpen La. RG24 7 G6
Milton Clo. RG24 6 C4
Minden Clo. RG24 6 D3
Mitchell Gdns. RG22 8 B5
Monarch Clo. RG22 11 E6
Mongers Piece. RG24 7 F1
Montague Pl. RG21 3 C5
Montserrat Clo. RG24 6 B3
Montserrat Rd. RG24 6 B3
Moor View. RG22 7 F6
Moorfoot Gdns. RG22 8 D2
Moorhams Av. RG22 11 E5
Morley Rd. RG21 9 H3
Morse Rd. RG22 5 F6
Mortimer La. RG21 3 A3
Mourne Clo. RG22 8 C1
Mozart Clo. RG22 9 F5
Mulberry Way. RG24 7 E1
Mullins Clo. RG21 6 B5
Munnings Clo. RG21 10 C4
Musgrave Clo. RG22 9 E5
Musket Copse. RG24 10 F1
Myland Clo. RG21 6 B5

Napoleon Dri. RG23 5 E3
Nash Clo. RG22 6 B6
Neath Rd. RG21 10 C2
Neville Clo. RG21 10 A5
New Market Sq. RG21 3 C2
New Rd. RG21 3 B4
New St. RG21 3 B3
Nightingale Gdns. RG24 4 D2
Norden Clo. RG21 10 A1
Normanton Rd. RG21 6 A5
Norn Hill. RG21 6 B6
Norn Hill Clo. RG21 6 B6
Northgate Way. RG22 11 E5
Norton Ride. RG24 7 E6
Norwich Clo. RG22 8 D5
Norwood Gdns. RG21 9 G3
Novello Clo. RG22 9 E6
Nursery Clo. RG24 7 E2

Oaklands Way. RG23 4 D4
Oakridge Rd. RG21 6 A5
Oakwood. RG24 7 E1
Ochil Clo. RG22 8 C1
Octavian Clo. RG22 11 F4
Old Basing Mall. RG21 3 B2
Old Common Rd. RG21 10 C3
Old Down Clo. RG22 8 B4
Old Kempshott La. RG22 8 B2
Old Reading Rd. RG21 3 D1
Old Worting Rd. RG22 4 D6

Oldberg Gdns. RG22 9 G5
Olivers Walk. RG24 7 E6
Onslow Clo. RG24 6 D4
Orchard Rd. RG22 8 D1
Orkney Clo. RG24 6 C4
Osbourne Clo. RG21 5 G3
Osprey Rd. RG22 8 B4
Oyster Clo. RG22 11 E5

Pack La. RG22 8 A2
Packenham Rd. RG21 9 G1
Paddock Rd. RG22 8 D1
Paddockfields. RG24 7 G5
Pages Bungalows. RG21 3 A3
Palmer Clo. RG21 6 B5
Park Av. RG24 11 F2
Park Gdns. RG21 10 C4
Park La. RG21 11 F2
Parkside Rd. RG21 3 D6
Parkwood Clo. RG24 7 E1
Paterson Clo. RG22 8 D5
Paulet Pl. RG24 11 G1
Paxton Clo. RG22 11 E4
Peake Clo. RG24 7 E6
Pelham Clo. RG24 11 G2
Pelton Rd. RG21 5 G4
Pembroke Rd. RG23 4 D5
Pemerton Rd. RG24 6 B6
Pendennis Clo. RG23 4 D4
Pennine Clo. RG22 8 C2
Pennine Way. RG22 8 C2
Penrith Rd. RG21 3 A4
Pentland Clo. RG22 8 C1
Pershore Rd. RG24 6 A4
Petersfield Clo. RG24 7 F1
Petrel Croft. RG22 8 B5
Pettys Brook Rd. RG24 7 E1
Petunia Clo. RG24 8 B5
Petworth Clo. RG22 11 F5
Peveral Walk. RG22 9 E1
Peveral Way. RG22 9 E2
Pheasant Clo. RG24 8 A4
Pheby Rd. RG22 9 E3
Phoenix Park Ter. RG21 10 A1
Pimpernel Clo. RG24 7 F1
Pinkerton Rd. RG22 8 D2
Pinnell Clo. RG22 11 E5
Pitcairn Clo. RG24 6 C3
Pitman Clo. RG24 8 D3
Pittard Rd. RG21 9 G1
Plover Clo. RG22 8 B3
Popley Way. RG24 5 G2
Poppy Fields. RG24 7 F5
Porchester Sq. RG21 3 B2
Portacre Rise. RG21 9 G1
Porter Rd. RG22 9 G4
Portsmouth Cres. RG22 9 E2
Portsmouth Walk. RG22 9 E2
Portsmouth Way. RG22 9 E2
Portway Pl. RG23 4 C5
Potters Walk. RG21 3 B3
Poynings Clo. RG21 10 B5
Priestley Rd. RG24 5 F3
Primrose Gdns. RG24 11 F6
Princes Cres. RG22 9 F2
Priory Gdns. RG24 7 G6
Privett Clo. RG24 7 F4
Purcell Clo. RG22 9 G4
Puttenham Rd. RG24 7 F2
Pyotts Copse. RG24 7 F4
Pyotts Ct. RG24 7 F3
Pyotts Hill. RG24 7 F3

Queen Annes Wk. RG21 3 C3
Queen Mary Av. RG21 3 A6
Queens Rd. RG21 5 G5
Quilter Rd. RG22 8 D4

Radford Gdns. RG21 9 G1
Radwick Clo. RG21 9 G1
Rainbow Clo. RG21 11 H2
Rainham Clo. RG22 8 B6
Rankine Rd. RG24 6 C5
Raphael Clo. RG21 10 D3
Ravel Clo. RG22 9 F4
Rayleigh Rd. RG21 3 A2
Reading Rd. RG21 6 C5
Red Lion La. RG21 3 C3
Redbridge La. RG24 10 D2
Remembrance Gdns. RG24
Rembrandt Clo. RG21 10 C3
Renoir Clo. RG21 10 C4
Renown Way. RG24 7 E1
Restormel Clo. RG23 4 D4
Reynolds Clo. RG21 10 D3
Ribble Way. RG21 10 C2
Richmond Rd. RG21 5 H4
Ridge Clo. RG22 11 G6
Riley La. RG24 7 G6
Ringway East. RG21 10 D1
Ringway North. RG21 5 F3

Ringway South. RG21 3 A6
Ringway West. RG21 5 F3
Riverside Clo. RG24 7 G5
Robin Clo. RG22 8 B4
Roding Clo. RG21 10 C2
Rochester Clo. RG22 8 D5
Rochford Rd. RG21 5 H5
Roentgen Rd. RG24 7 E6
Roman Rd. RG23 4 C6
Roman Way. RG23 4 B6
Romsey Clo. RG24 5 H2
Rooksdown Av. RG24 4 D2
Rooksdown La. RG24 4 D2
Rose Clo. RG22 8 C5
Rose Hodson Pl. RG23 4 D3
Roseberry Clo. RG24 8 C6
Rosehip Way. RG24 7 F4
Ross Clo. RG21 9 H3
Rossini Clo. RG22 9 F5
Rothay Ct. RG21 10 C2
Roundmead Rd. RG21 5 H6
Royal Clo. RG21 11 E6
Rubens Clo. RG21 10 C4
Ruskin Clo. RG21 10 D4
Russell Rd. RG21 3 C6
Rutherford Rd. RG24 11 G4

Saffron Clo. RG24 7 F1
St Andrews Rd. RG22 9 E2
St Christophers Clo. RG22 8 A1
St Davids Rd. RG22 8 C5
St Gabriels Lea. RG24 7 F2
St Johns Walk. RG21 3 B2
St Leonards Av. RG24 7 F2
St Marys Ct. RG21 3 D2
St Michaels Rd. RG25 5 D2
St Patricks Rd. RG22 9 F2
St Pauls Rd. RG22 9 F1
St Peters Rd. RG22 8 D1
St Thomas Clo. RG21 5 H4
Salisbury Gdns. RG22 9 E1
Sandbanks Dri. RG22 11 F4
Sandpiper Way. RG22 8 A5
Sandringham Ct. RG22 9 F1
Sandys Clo. RG22 9 F1
Sandys Rd. RG22 9 F1
Sarum Hill. RG21 3 A3
Saxon Way. RG24 7 E6
Scharlatti Rd. RG22 9 G5
Schubert Rd. RG22 9 F5
Scotney Rd. RG21 10 A5
Seagull Clo. RG22 8 B5
Seal Rd. RG21 3 C3
Selby Walk. RG24 6 A4
Severn Way. RG21 10 C2
Seymour Rd. RG22 8 D3
Shakespeare Rd. RG24 6 B4
Shelley Clo. RG24 6 C5
Sheppard Rd. RG21 9 G3
Sheraton Av. RG22 11 F4
Sherborne Rd. RG21 5 H3
Sherrington Way. RG22 9 G3
Sherwood Clo. RG22 11 G5
Shetland Rd. RG24 6 B3
Shipton Way. RG22 8 D3
Shooters Way. RG21 6 B6
Sibelius Clo. RG22 9 F5
Sidlaw Clo. RG22 8 C2
Silvester Clo. RG21 10 C2
Simmons Walk. RG24 7 E3
Simons Clo. RG24 6 D3
Simons Rd. RG24 6 D3
Skippets Lane E. RG21 10 B5
Skippets Lane W. RG21 10 B5
Snowdrop Clo. RG24 8 B5
Solbys Rd. RG21 5 H5
Solent Dri. RG22 11 F4
Sonning Clo. RG22 8 B6
Soper Gro. RG21 10 A1
Sorrells Clo. RG24 7 E2
South Ham Rd. RG22 9 F1
Southend Rd. RG21 3 A2
Southern Rd. RG21 3 B4
Southlands. RG24 6 D2
Sperrin Clo. RG22 8 C2
Stag Hill. RG22 9 E2
Stag Oak La. RG24 6 D1
Stanford Rd. RG22 8 D5
Starling Clo. RG22 8 B4
Station App. RG21 3 B1
Station Hill. RG21 3 B1
Station Mall. RG21 3 B1
Station Rd. RG25 9 H6
Stephenson Rd. RG21 5 F4
Stewart Rd. RG21 6 D4
Stockbridge Clo. RG22 7 F1
Stocker Clo. RG21 10 A5
Stratfield Rd. RG21 6 A5
Stratton Rd. RG22 9 G3
Strauss Rd. RG22 8 D4
Stravinsky Rd. RG22 9 G5

Stroud Clo. RG24 6 D3
Stroudley Rd. RG24 6 D5
Stubbs Rd. RG21 10 C5
Stukeley Rd. RG21 5 G6
Sullivan Rd. RG22 9 F4
Summerfield. RG24 7 F1
Sunflower Clo. RG22 8 C5
Sutton Rd. RG21 6 A6
Swallow Clo. RG22 8 B4
Swing Swang La. RG24 6 D5
Sycamore Way. RG23 5 E3
Sylvia Clo. RG21 3 A5

Tallis Gdns. RG22 9 F4
Tamarisk Clo. RG22 11 G6
Tangway. RG24 7 E1
Tasmania Clo. RG24 6 B3
Taverner Clo. RG21 6 C6
Teal Cres. RG22 8 A5
Telford Rd. RG21 5 F4
Tennyson Way. RG22 9 F2
Test Way. RG22 10 C2
Tewkesbury Clo. RG24 6 A4
Thames Ct. RG21 10 C2
The Brackens. RG22 11 G5
The Confields. RG22 11 G4
The Croft. RG22 11 G5
The Danes. RG22 3 C2
The Dell. RG25 11 H2
The Glebe. RG21 3 B2
The Harrow Way. RG22 9 F3
The Hedgerows. RG24 7 F4
The Laurels. RG21 6 C6
The Mead. RG24 11 G1
The Meadow. RG22 11 G6
The Street. RG22 7 F6
The Topiary. RG24 7 F4
The Wolds. RG22 8 D2
The Woodlands. RG24 7 F1
Thornhill Way. RG24 7 F1
Thrush Clo. RG22 8 B4
Thumwood. RG24 7 E2
Thyme Clo. RG24 7 E1
Tiberius Clo. RG23 4 D3
Timberlake Rd. RG21 3 A2
Timor Clo. RG24 6 B3
Tintagel Clo. RG23 4 D4
Tintern Clo. RG24 5 G2
Tippet Gdns. RG22 9 G5
Tiverton Rd. RG23 4 C6
Tobago Clo. RG24 6 A3
Tollway. RG24 7 F1
Townsend Clo. RG21 5 G6
Trellis Dri. RG24 7 F4
Trent Way. RG21 10 C2
Trinidad Clo. RG24 6 A4
Tulip Clo. RG22 8 C5
Turner Clo. RG21 10 D3
Tweedsmuir Clo. RG22 8 D1

Upfallow. RG24 7 F5
Upper Chestnut Dri. RG21 9 G2
Upper Sherborne Rd. RG21 5 G3
Upronfield Clo. RG22 11 F4
Upton Cres. RG21 5 H3

Van Dyck Clo. RG21 10 D3
Vanburgh Gdns. RG22 11 F4
Verdi Clo. RG22 9 E5
Veronica Clo. RG22 8 C5
Viables La. RG22 10 A5
Victoria Pl. RG22 4 C6
Victoria St. RG21 3 B4
Violet Clo. RG22 8 B6
Vivian Rd. RG21 6 B6
Vyne Rd. RG21 3 B1

Wade Rd. RG24 6 D4
Wagner Clo. RG22 9 F5
Wallins Copse. RG24 7 E3
Wallis Ct. RG23 5 E4
Wallis Rd. RG21 3 B5
Wallop Dri. RG22 11 E5
Warbleton Rd. RG24 7 F2
Warren Way. RG22 9 E1
Warton Rd. RG24 10 B1
Warwick Rd. RG23 4 D5
Wateridge Rd. RG21 6 B5
Waterloo Av. RG23 4 D3
Watling End. RG21 11 F4
Watson Way. RG23 5 E4
Wavell Clo. RG22 9 F2
Waverley Av. RG22 9 H2
Wayside Rd. RG23 4 C5
Weale Ct. RG21 10 A1
Webb Clo. RG24 7 E2
Wella Path. RG21 3 B5
Wella Rd. RG21 9 G3
Wellington Ter. RG23 4 D3
Wesley Walk. RG21 3 B2

Wessex Clo. RG21 9 H1
West Ham Clo. RG22 5 E6
West Ham La, Worting Rd. RG23 4 C6
West Ham La, Grafton Way. RG22 5 E6
Westbrook Ct. RG23 4 C6
Western Way. RG22 9 F1
Westfield Rd. RG21 3 D6
Westgate Clo. RG23 4 C5
Westminster Clo. RG22 8 C5
Westray Clo. RG21 6 C6
Westside Clo. RG22 9 E2
Weysprings Clo. RG21 10 C2
Whistler Clo. RG21 10 C4
White Hart La. RG21 3 D4
Whitehead Clo. RG24 7 E6
Whitestones. RG22 11 G5
Whitewood. RG24 7 E2
Whitney Rd. RG24 6 D6
Wicklow Ct. RG22 8 C1
Widmore Rd. RG24 8 D3
Wights Walk. RG22 11 F4
Willoughby Way. RG24 5 E4
Willow Way. RG23 5 E3
Wilmot Way. RG23 5 E4
Wilton Pl. RG21 5 G6
Winchcombe Rd. RG21 5 H6
Winchester Rd, Basingstoke. RG21 3 A5
Winchester Rd, Kempshott. RG22 8 B6
Winchester St. RG21 3 B4
Windermere Av. RG22 8 C3
Windrush Clo. RG21 10 C2
Windsor Gdns. RG22 11 E5
Winklebury Way. RG23 4 C5
Winterthur Way. RG21 3 A1
Winton Sq. RG21 3 B4
Woburn Gdns. RG22 9 E1
Wood Clo. RG22 11 F5
Woodbury Rd. RG22 11 F4
Woodgarston Dri. RG22 11 E5
Woodmere Croft. RG22 8 B6
Woodpecker Clo. RG22 8 A5
Woodroffe Dri. RG22 8 D3
Woods La. RG25 9 F6
Woodside Gdns. RG24 7 E1
Woodstock Mead. RG22 11 F6
Woodville Clo. RG24 7 E2
Woodville La. RG24 7 E2
Woolford Way. RG23 5 E5
Worcester Av. RG22 8 C5
Wordsworth Clo. RG24 6 B5
Worting Rd. RG21 3 A3
Wote St. RG21 3 C3
Wrekin Clo. RG22 8 C1
Wykeham Dri. RG23 4 C6

York Clo. RG22 8 D5

Zinnia Clo. RG22 8 B6

HEATH END/ TADLEY

Abbotswood Clo. RG26 13 E5
Adam Clo. RG26 12 C2
Almswood Rd. RG26 12 D2
Ambrose Rd. RG26 13 E3
Appleshaw Clo. RG26 13 E3
Arnwood Av. RG26 13 G3
Ash La. RG26 12 B3
Ashurst Clo. RG26 12 D4
Barlows Rd. RG26 13 E4
Baughurst Rd. RG26 12 B3
Beavers Clo. RG26 12 D3
Binley Ct. RG26 13 F3
Birch Rd. RG26 12 C2
Bishops Clo. RG26 12 D2
Bishopswood La. RG26 12 B3
Bishopswood Rd. RG26 12 C3
Blakes La. RG26 13 E3
Bordon Clo. RG26 12 D4
Bowmonts Rd. RG26 13 E4
Brackenwood Dri. RG26 12 D2
Bramdean Clo. RG26 13 G4
Brampton Mdw. RG26 13 G4
Briar Way. RG26 13 F3
Brimpton Rd. RG26 12 A2
Broadhalfpenny La. RG26 13 F2
Broadoak. RG26 13 G3
Brook Grn. RG26 13 G4
Brookside Walk. RG26 13 G3
Burney Bit. RG26 13 G3
Burnham Rd. RG26 12 C2
Burnley Clo. RG26 13 E4
Candover Clo. RG26 13 E4
Carrington Cres. RG26 13 E3

Cedar Clo. RG26	13 G5	Oak Tree Clo. RG26	13 E3
Cheriton Clo. RG26	13 E4	Oakfield Rd. RG26	13 H2
Chippendale Clo. RG26	12 B2	Odette Gdns. RG26	13 E3
Christy Ct. RG26	13 E4	Otterbourne Cres. RG26	13 E5
Church Brook. RG26	12 D5	Pamber Heath Rd. RG26	13 G4
Church Rd,		Pelican Rd. RG26	13 G2
Pamber Heath. RG26	13 G2	Pinehurst. RG26	13 E4
Church Rd,		Pinewood Clo. RG26	12 A2
Tadley. RG26	13 E5	Pinks La. RG26	12 B2
Churchill Clo. RG26	13 G5	Plantation Rd. RG26	12 C2
Clapps Gate Rd. RG26	13 H2	Pleasant Hill. RG26	13 E3
Conifer Clo. RG26	12 B2	Poplar Clo. RG26	12 B3
Coppice Clo. RG26	12 B3	Portiswood Clo. RG26	13 G3
Crookham Clo. RG26	13 E5	Portway. RG26	12 B2
Deanswood Rd. RG26	12 D3	Purbrook Rd. RG26	12 D4
Denmead. RG26	13 E4	Ramsdell Clo. RG26	13 E4
Douro. RG26	12 B3	Rectory Clo. RG26	13 F5
Droxford Cres. RG26	12 D4	Reubens Cres. RG26	13 E3
Eastlyn Rd. RG26	13 H3	Reynards Clo. RG26	13 E3
Elmhurst. RG26	13 E4	Rimes La. RG26	12 C5
Fairlawn Rd. RG26	13 F5	Romans Gate. RG26	13 H2
Fairoak Way. RG26	12 B2	Ropley Clo. RG26	12 D4
Falcon Fields. RG26	13 E2	Rosebank Clo. RG26	13 E3
Farringdon Way. RG26	13 E4	Rotherwick Rd. RG26	13 E5
Finch Clo. RG26	13 F4	Rowan Clo. RG26	13 F4
Forest Clo. RG26	12 B2	Rowan Rd. RG26	13 F4
Forest La. RG26	13 G5	St Peters Clo. RG26	13 E5
Franklin Av. RG26	12 D2	Sandford Rd. RG26	12 D3
Fullerton Way. RG26	13 F4	Sandy La. RG26	13 G4
Furze Rd. RG26	12 C2	Sarisbury Clo. RG26	12 D4
Georgina Gdns. RG26	13 G3	Sarum Rd. RG26	12 D2
Giles Ct. RG26	13 F4	Selbourne Walk. RG26	12 D4
Giles Rd. RG26	13 F3	Shaw La. RG26	12 C5
Glebe Clo. RG26	13 F5	Sheridan Cres. RG26	12 B3
Glendale Rd. RG26	12 D3	Shyshack La. RG26	12 B2
Gorselands. RG26	13 E3	Silchester Rd. RG26	13 E2
Gravelly Clo. RG26	13 E5	Silverdale Rd. RG26	13 E3
Greywell Clo. RG26	12 D3	Skates La. RG26	13 F6
Gutteridge La. RG26	12 D4	Southdown Rd. RG26	12 D3
Hamble Dri. RG26	13 G3	Spencer Clo. RG26	13 G2
Hanger Rd. RG26	12 C2	Spiers Clo. RG26	13 F4
Harmsworth Rd. RG26	13 E3	Springfield Rd. RG26	13 H2
Hartley Gdns. RG26	13 E5	Stanfield. RG26	13 E4
Hartshill Rd. RG26	12 C3	Stephens Rd. RG26	13 F4
Hawkley Dri. RG26	13 F4	Stratfield Av. RG26	13 E4
Hazel Grn. RG26	12 A3	Stratfield Ct. RG26	13 F4
Heath Clo. RG26	12 B2	Stroud Clo. RG26	13 G2
Heath End Rd. RG26	12 B3	Swains Clo. RG26	13 E3
Heath Rd. RG26	13 G3	Swains Rd. RG26	13 E3
Heather Dri. RG26	12 C2	Swanwick Walk. RG26	13 E3
Heathlands. RG26	13 E5	Sympson Rd. RG26	13 G3
Heathrow Copse. RG26	12 A3	Tadley Common Rd.	
Hedge End. RG26	13 F5	RG26	13 F2
Hepplewhite Clo. RG26	12 B2	Tadley Hill. RG26	13 F4
Herriard Way. RG26	13 E4	The Glen. RG26	13 H3
Hillcrest. RG26	13 E3	The Green. RG26	13 F5
Hinton Clo. RG26	13 E4	The Hawthorns. RG26	12 B3
Honeybottom Rd. RG26	12 C3	The Lane. RG26	13 E2
Huntsmoor Rd. RG26	13 F3	The Oaks. RG26	12 D4
Hylton Clo. RG26	13 E4	The Old Forge. RG26	12 B3
Hythe Clo. RG26	13 E4	The Orchard. RG26	13 F3
Ilex Clo. RG26	13 H2	The Warren. RG26	12 D4
Impstone La. RG26	13 H2	Titchfield Clo. RG26	13 E5
INDUSTRIAL ESTATES:		Tomlins Clo. RG26	13 E4
Calleva Pk Ind Est.		Tudor Ct. RG26	13 E3
RG26	12 B1	Tunworth Mews. RG26	13 F4
Inhurst Way. RG26	12 C3	Valley Way. RG26	13 H2
Jubilee Clo. RG26	13 G2	Vinetree Clo. RG26	13 G4
Knapp La. RG26	13 G5	Violet La. RG26	12 A4
Knollys Clo. RG26	13 H2	Wakeford Clo. RG26	13 H2
Lake Ct. RG26	13 G4	Wakeford Rd. RG26	13 H2
Lamdens Walk. RG26	13 E4	Warblington Clo. RG26	13 F4
Linton Clo. RG26	13 F5	Wellington Cres. RG26	12 B3
Long Gro. RG26	13 F5	West St. RG26	13 F3
Main Rd. RG26	13 F5	Westfield Clo. RG26	13 G3
Malthouse La. RG26	13 F5	Westlyn Rd. RG26	13 G3
Manse La. RG26	13 E4	Weyhill Clo. RG26	13 E5
Maple Gro. RG26	13 G6	Whitedown Rd. RG26	12 C3
Mariners Clo. RG26	12 D2	Wickham Clo. RG26	13 E3
Meon Clo. RG26	13 E3	Wigmore Rd. RG26	12 C2
Millers Rd. RG26	13 E5	Wildmoor Dri. RG26	12 B3
Minstead Clo. RG26	13 E5	Willow Rd. RG26	13 E4
Monkswood Cres. RG26	13 E5	Winchfield Gdns. RG26	13 E4
Mornington Clo. RG26	12 B3	Winkworth La. RG26	13 E2
Mortimer Gdns. RG26	13 E3	Winston Av. RG26	13 G4
Mount Pleasant. RG26	12 A3	Wolverton Rd. RG26	12 A4
Mount Pleasant Dri.		Woodlands Rd. RG26	12 A2
RG26	12 D3		
Mulfords Hill. RG26	13 E2		
New Church Rd. RG26	12 D3		
New Rd. RG26	12 C4		
Newtown. RG26	12 D3		
Northview Rd. RG26	13 F5		
Oak Clo. RG26	12 A3		

KINGSCLERE

Anchor Rd. RG20	14 C3		
Ash Grove. RG20	14 D2		
Basingstoke Rd. RG20	14 D2		

Bear Hill. RG20	14 B3	Grub La. RG23	15 C5
Brimley Hill Ct. RG20	14 C3	Hamble Clo. RG23	15 C3
Brimpton Rd. RG20	14 D2	Hazel Clo. RG23	15 D4
Bushnells Dri. RG20	14 D2	Highland Dri. RG23	15 B2
Byfields Rd. RG20	14 C2	Hill Rd. RG23	15 B2
Canons Clo. RG20	14 B2	Hoopers Way. RG23	15 C4
Cedar Dri. RG20	14 D2	Hunters Clo. RG23	15 D3
Coppice Rd. RG20	14 D2	Itchen Clo. RG23	15 D3
Cottington Clo. RG20	14 D3	Kennet Way. RG23	15 C3
Ecchinswell Rd. RG20	14 A2	Kings Orchard. RG23	15 C4
Elm Gro. RG20	14 D2	Kintyre Clo. RG23	15 C4
Elm Grove Farm. RG20	14 D2	Lightsfield. RG23	15 C2
Elm Grove Flats. RG20	14 D2	Link Way. RG23	15 C4
Fawconer Rd. RG20	14 B2	Litton Gdns. RG23	15 C3
Felden Ct. RG20	14 B2	Lomond Clo. RG23	15 B3
Foxs La. RG20	14 B3	Longfield. RG23	15 C2
Frogs Hole. RG20	14 B2	Lyde Clo. RG23	15 B2
Garden Clo. RG20	14 D3	Malshanger La. RG23	15 B2
Garrett Clo. RG20	14 B2	Marlborough Gdns.	
George St. RG20	14 C2	RG23	15 C3
Greenacre. RG20	14 D2	Matthews Way. RG23	15 D4
Greenlands Rd. RG20	14 D2	Medina Gdns. RG23	15 C4
Hardys Field. RG20	14 B1	Medway Av. RG23	15 D3
Highams Clo. RG20	14 D3	Meon Rd. RG23	15 B3
Hollowshot La. RG20	14 B4	Mull Clo. RG23	15 D4
Hook Rd. RG20	14 E3	Oak Clo. RG23	15 C4
INDUSTRIAL ESTATES:		Oakley La. RG23	15 B4
Kingsclere Park		Oban Clo. RG23	15 B3
Ind Est. RG20	14 B1	Pack La. RG23	15 C3
Keeps Mead. RG20	14 B1	Park Clo. RG23	15 C3
Kevin Clo. RG20	14 F3	Petersfield. RG23	15 A3
King John Rd. RG20	14 D3	Rectory Rd. RG23	15 C5
Knowle Cres. RG20	14 D3	Sainfoin La. RG23	15 C5
Larch Dri. RG20	14 C3	St Johns Piece. RG23	15 C5
Link Rd. RG20	14 E2	St Johns Rd. RG23	15 D2
Longcroft Rd. RG20	14 B1	Severn Gdns. RG23	15 C4
Love La. RG20	14 A2	Springfield. RG23	15 D3
Newbury Rd. RG20	14 B1	Station Rd. RG23	15 A3
North St. RG20	14 C2	Stour Rd. RG23	15 C4
Peel Gdns. RG20	14 B1	Sunny Mead. RG23	15 C5
Pennys Hatch. RG20	14 E2	Tamar Clo. RG23	15 D3
Phoenix Ct. RG20	14 C2	Tanners Way. RG23	15 C3
Popes Hill. RG20	14 B2	The Drive. RG23	15 C4
Poveys Mead. RG20	14 E3	The Vale. RG23	15 C2
Priors Clo. RG20	14 D2	Tollgate Clo. RG23	15 C2
Queens Rd. RG20	14 E3	Turnpike Way. RG23	15 B2
Rose Hodson Ct. RG20	14 B1	Upper Farm Rd. RG23	15 C5
St Marys Rd. RG20	14 C3	Water Ridges. RG23	15 C4
Sandford Clo. RG20	14 F3	Westbrook Clo. RG23	15 C5
South Rd. RG20	14 E2	Wither Rise. RG23	15 C4
Sunnyside. RG20	14 B3	Yew Tree Clo. RG23	15 C5
Swan St. RG20	14 B3		
The Dell. RG20	14 D2		

OVERTON

The Lines. RG20	14 C1		
The Paddock. RG20	14 B2		
Thorneley Rd. RG20	14 D2	Alexander Rd. RG25	16 C4
Tower Hill. RG20	14 B2	Battens La. RG25	16 C4
Tower Hill Ct. RG20	14 B4	Beech Clo. RG25	16 C2
Union La. RG20	14 C1	Beech Gro. RG25	16 C2
Wellmans Mdw. RG20	14 B1	Berrydown La. RG25	16 D5
Winchester Rd. RG20	14 B4	Bridge St. RG25	16 B4
Yew Clo. RG20	14 E3	Charledown Clo. RG25	16 B5

OAKLEY

		Charledown Rd. RG25	16 B5
		Church Rd. RG25	16 B3
Andover Rd. RG23	15 A2	Copse Rd. RG25	16 B5
Anton Clo. RG23	15 C3	Court Drove. RG25	16 A1
Apple Tree Clo. RG23	15 C5	Crawts Rd. RG25	16 B5
Arran Clo. RG23	15 B2	Dellands. RG25	16 B4
Ash Tree Clo. RG23	15 B5	Dellands La. RG25	16 B4
Aviemore Dri. RG23	15 B3	Elm Rd. RG25	16 C2
Avon Rd. RG23	15 B3	Foxdown. RG25	16 C2
Barn La. RG23	15 B5	Glebe Meadow. RG25	16 B3
Barra Clo. RG23	15 B2	Greyhound La. RG25	16 B4
Beech Tree Clo. RG23	15 B5	Harveys Field. RG25	16 B4
Blackwater Clo. RG23	15 C4	High St. RG25	16 B2
Boon Way. RG23	15 B2	Hill Meadow. RG25	16 B2
Braemar Clo. RG23	15 B3	Hilltop Rd. RG25	16 C2
Cadnam Clo. RG23	15 C3	Kerchers Field. RG25	16 B4
Caithness Clo. RG23	15 B3	Kingsclere Rd. RG25	16 B1
Cedar Tree Clo. RG23	15 C5	Lambs Clo. RG25	16 C3
Croft Rd. RG23	15 C4	Lion Clo. RG25	16 B4
Dellfield. RG23	15 D1	London Rd. RG25	16 C4
Dever Clo. RG23	15 C5	Lordsfield Gdns. RG25	16 B3
Fairview Mdw. RG23	15 C5	Mede Clo. RG25	16 C4
Fox La. RG23	15 D2	Nightingale Rise. RG25	16 C4
Foxmoor Clo. RG23	15 D1	Oak Clo. RG25	16 B4
Frome Clo. RG23	15 C2	Papermakers. RG25	16 C4
Glamis Clo. RG23	15 C2	Pond Clo. RG25	16 B5
Goddards Firs. RG23	15 D4	Poultons Clo. RG25	16 B5
Greenaways. RG23	15 D3	Poultons Rd. RG25	16 B5
		Pound Rd. RG25	16 C5
		Poyntz Rd. RG25	16 B4
		Red Lion La. RG25	16 B4
		Riverside Clo. RG25	16 C3

Sapley La. RG25	16 B4		
Silk Mill La. RG25	16 A4		
Southington Clo. RG25	16 A4		
Southington La. RG25	16 A4		
Sprents La. RG25	16 C4		
Station Hill. RG25	16 C2		
Station Rd. RG25	16 C4		
The Green. RG25	16 C4		
The Lynch. RG25	16 A3		
The Orchard. RG25	16 C4		
Two Gate La. RG25	16 C4		
Two Gate Mdw. RG25	16 C4		
Vinns La. RG25	16 A4		
Waltham Ct. RG25	16 C4		
Waltham Rd. RG25	16 C4		
Winchester St. RG25	16 C4		
Woodlands. RG25	16 B4		

WHITCHURCH

Alliston Way. RG28	17 C5		
Andover Rd. RG28	17 A5		
Ardglen Rd. RG28	17 B3		
Bell St. RG28	17 B3		
Bell Yard. RG28	17 B3		
Bellevue. RG28	17 B3		
Bere Hill. RG28	17 C1		
Bere Hill Clo. RG28	17 C2		
Bicester Clo. RG28	17 B2		
Blosswood Dri. RG28	17 A2		
Blosswood La. RG28	17 A2		
Boundary Clo. RG28	17 B3		
Broadway. RG28	17 C4		
Brooks Clo. RG28	17 D5		
Charlcot Clo. RG28	17 C6		
Charlcot Farm. RG28	17 C3		
Chatter La. RG28	17 C3		
Church St. RG28	17 B4		
Clemence Gdns. RG28	17 B3		
Dances La. RG28	17 C2		
Daniel Rd. RG28	17 D4		
Evingar Gdns. RG28	17 B2		
Fair Clo. RG28	17 B4		
Fairfield. RG28	17 C2		
Firs Way. RG28	17 B4		
Great La. RG28	17 B4		
Greenwoods. RG28	17 C1		
Hartley Meadow. RG28	17 B3		
Hides Clo. RG28	17 C4		
Jobson Clo. RG28	17 C5		
Kingfisher Clo. RG28	17 C3		
Kings Walk. RG28	17 C3		
Kingsley Park. RG28	17 B2		
Laundry Yd. RG28	17 B3		
London St. RG28	17 C3		
Longs Ct. RG28	17 B4		
Lower Evingar Rd. RG28	17 B3		
Lynch Hill. RG28	17 C2		
Lynch Hill Park. RG28	17 C2		
Mann Clo. RG28	17 C2		
McFauld Way. RG28	17 C1		
Meadow View. RG28	17 A1		
Micheldever Clo. RG28	17 D6		
Micheldever Rd. RG28	17 C5		
Neuvic Way. RG28	17 D5		
Newbury St. RG28	17 C4		
Oakland Rd. RG28	17 B3		
Orchard Pl. RG28	17 B3		
Pages Yard. RG28	17 B3		
Pesthouse La. RG28	17 B3		
Pound Meadow. RG28	17 B3		
Queens Rd. RG28	17 D3		
Rampton Clo. RG28	17 D4		
Sheppard Clo. RG28	17 C3		
Station App. RG28	17 C3		
Station Rd. RG28	17 C3		
Test Mews. RG28	17 C3		
Test Rd. RG28	17 C3		
The Green. RG28	17 D4		
The Knowlings. RG28	17 D4		
The Lynch. RG28	17 B3		
The Rookery. RG28	17 C4		
The Weir. RG28	17 B4		
Town Mill La. RG28	17 C4		
Upper Evingar Rd. RG28	17 B3		
Webbs Farm Clo. RG28	17 C1		
Wells La. RG28	17 B4		
Wheeler Clo. RG28	17 D4		
Whitchurch By-Pass.			
RG28	17 A4		
Winchester Rd. RG28	17 B5		